Private Capital for New Towns

PAPERS DELIVERED AT A CONFERENCE
FOR ECONOMISTS, TOWN PLANNERS,
AND INSTITUTIONAL INVESTORS

A. G. LING
JAMES ROUSE
W. A. WEST
MARIAN BOWLEY
NATHANIEL LICHFIELD

with a Preface by

F. G. PENNANCE

Published by
THE INSTITUTE OF ECONOMIC AFFAIRS
1969

First published March 1969
by
THE INSTITUTE OF ECONOMIC AFFAIRS
© 1969

255   69645-0

Printed in Great Britain by
THE SOMAN-WHERRY PRESS LTD., NORWICH
Set in Monotype Plantin series 110

CONTENTS

Foreword

As part of its educational purpose in explaining the light that economics can throw on business and public policy, the Institute re-prints as *Occasional Papers* essays or lectures judged of interest to a wider audience than that to which they were originally addressed. *Occasional Paper* 26 comprises a selection of Papers first delivered at a conference on Private Enterprise and New Towns in London on 23 October, 1968 and chaired by Professor Arthur G. Ling, President of the Town Planning Institute.

The main paper was delivered by Mr James Rouse of America who spoke from his experience in establishing a new town with capital raised from private sources. Aspects of the subject were considered in other papers by Professor Marian Bowley, Professor Nathaniel Lichfield and Professor W. A. West.

To introduce the subject and indicate aspects of special interest to economists, we have invited Mr F. G. Pennance, Head of the Economics Department of the College of Estate Management, to write a Preface.

The *Paper* is published as of special value for teachers and students of economics, but it will also be of interest to town planners, users of the large investible funds assembled by insurance companies, pension funds, and other large investors, and not least to policy-makers in government and industry concerned about the reasons why private capital is put into offices and shops but rarely into new housing to let, hospitals or schools.

January 1969   EDITOR

Preface

F. G. PENNANCE

Head of the Economics Department, College of Estate Management
(University of Reading)

New Towns are now a well-established part of the British scene. The original 14 areas 'designated' under the New Towns Act of 1946 have now grown to almost twice that number, with more currently under review. The earlier projections of small self-contained towns of 50,000 to 70,000 persons have been revised upwards and more-recently designated areas envisage much larger complexes of up to a quarter-million or more persons. After two decades or so of implementation the new towns' population still totals only about half-a-million; their 150,000 houses represent only $2\frac{1}{2}$ per cent of post-war house-building; only the towns on the London periphery (and not all of them) have begun to show a revenue surplus despite subsidies and favourable terms for finance, and criticisms have been voiced both of the rate of progress and of the lack of amenity in some areas.

The development of each new town rests with a semi-independent Development Corporation which, subject to general Ministerial control over planning, building and finance, is responsible for development and management up to the stage when a town's assets can be transferred as a 'going concern' either to the area local authority or (the present temporary solution) to a government-appointed holding and management agency—the Commission for the New Towns. However right they may have seemed in the economic atmosphere of the immediate post-war period, these arrangements have come under critical scrutiny in recent years. Ministerial and departmental controls—particularly over finance in times of economic stringency—have been blamed for hold-ups, imbalance between different sectors of town development, and cheeseparing on general amenities. Inevitably the necessity for exchequer financing and government control of this kind has begun to be questioned: given the ultimate prospect of a commercial rate of return on the whole investment, could not private initiative, enterprise and finance produce better results than the present system? What impediments stand in the way? Even within the present system, is there scope for improvement by more reliance on private enterprise?

In Britain, testing the hypothesis that entire towns can be developed profitably by private enterprise is still at a rudimentary stage. In the USA, by contrast, the city of Columbia, midway between Baltimore and Washington, is well under way. Conceived, planned, financed and implemented by private enterprise as a profitable venture without benefit of public aid or land acquisition, indeed in the teeth of unfavourable zoning laws, it has since 1963 made remarkable progress towards its goal of a city of 100,000 population by 1980. Mr James W. Rouse, whose address on Columbia constitutes a major contribution in this selection of conference papers, has played a leading role in the city's development from its incunabula as a logical extension of the large-scale urban developments in which his company had previously specialised. His historical and descriptive survey underlines the differences in approach and method between Columbia and the British new towns. He shows that a market-oriented approach not only need be no barrier to, but can form a sound basis for, the achievement of wider 'social' goals in urban design, that the price mechanism allied with voluntary co-operation is capable of balancing community needs with individual wants and individual participation in an effective way without the discouragement to imagination, initiative and resourcefulness that is often the price of government intervention and control.

Mr Rouse's account of Columbia, together with some of the questions and answers that accompanied it, is followed by three commentaries on the British scene. Professor W. A. West's paper on 'Planning' contrasts the advantages derived by Development Corporations from statutory protection and fiscal and financial discrimination with the handicaps with which they (especially the planning code) confront the private developer. The sheltered treatment of new towns, he believes, is poorly reflected in their economic performance, and he sees considerable merit in jettisoning a good deal of the present legislative planning machinery to permit market forces to work more freely.

Professor Marian Bowley, on the other hand, in her paper on 'Constraints on the Freedom of the Profit Motive' considers that wider economic and social issues must constrain the ability of the profit motive to provide a satisfactory answer to new town develop-

[6]

ment. New towns in Britain do not simply add to the housing stock in the most desirable forms and locations; they also serve urban renewal and regional rehabilitation growth policies. These would probably suffer under a system which permitted private enterprise to skim off the cream, leaving unprofitable housing and locations to public agencies. Professor Bowley's caveats are probably justified in the context of existing housing policy in Britain, although the gap between her views and Professor West's on this score might be narrowed were housing aid to be given more in the form of personal allowances to the needy and less in the form of publicly-provided subsidised housing. Even so, she would see possible clashes between public and private interest arising from differing attitudes towards futurity and social costs and the wider use of private enterprise must rest on more explicit recognition of such areas of conflict.

Professor Lichfield's paper on 'Private Capital in New Towns' doubts whether any new town can ever be wholly financed and developed profitably by private enterprise. Some parts—the 'infra-structure' and some public amenities—he considers must inevitably fall to be financed out of taxes; these apart, he sees no evidence in the experience of British new towns to deny a wider profitable role to private enterprise. He sees profit-sharing partnership arrangements between private and public developers as a prag-matic solution offering numerous side-benefits, and would extend some of the statutory, fiscal and financial advantages enjoyed by development corporations to private enterprise.

Although agreeing in many particulars with Mr Rouse, in one respect Professor Lichfield sits on the opposite side of the fence. He sees merit in the system of leasehold tenure as a way in which a town authority can maintain control over land use and share in rising rents. The Columbia venture, on the other hand, is based on freehold sales. Arguments can be advanced on both sides and there is probably no clear-cut answer; but public ownership of the freehold is rarely a necessary condition for land-use control and there may be more equitable ways of raising public revenues than from rising ground rents, despite the attraction to local authorities of such apparently independent sources of future finance. Neither is it necessarily true—as is sometimes argued—that financial partnership arrangements of this kind between developer and local authority are likely to promote more general or social amenities than any other. If such amenities (for example, parking facilities in a downtown area) are provided, they could be paid for by local taxation (abated by any general rate support grant), by charging developers higher ground rents, or by direct charges on users. In each case the burden of payment will be distributed differently and there is nothing to say the second alternative is any better than the others. On the other hand, there is some presumption that users' willingness to pay offers a better guide to overall efficiency in the allocation of resources than other systems. Efficiency in the use of resources is also a reason for viewing with suspicion the argument that developers should welcome partnership arrangements as a means of minimising the likelihood of competition from other developers, or that the long-term interests of the urban community are likely to be best served by what Professor West has called 'the new mortmain' of public landholding.

Undoubtedly the main issue touched on in this stimulating collection of Papers is this question of the financing of land uses in the protean mixture that comprises a town. For some, such as roads and main services, there may be no practical alternative to tax-financing. Others, whose form and content are determined directly by market demands, are generally priced—although the nature and extent of demand may be heavily influenced by the amount and character of government-channelled subsidy (e.g. housing). Between these limits lies a no-man's land—a range of social or 'community' uses capable of being tax-financed but for for which finance by some form of direct user-charge may be both possible and economic. One of the merits of the Columbia experiment from the standpoint of British experience has been to indicate and emphasise some of the possibilities for more use of prices and private enterprise to decide the allocation of land resources, not only within this range of 'social' uses, but also in the provision of lower-cost housing for rent.

More willingness in the UK to re-examine the possibilities of extending land-use pricing, for reform of housing subsidies, for a more flexible attitude towards new housing standards, could do much to widen the scope for private enterprise participation not only in new town development but across the whole spectrum of urban renewal.

I. Introduction

A. G. LING

*Professor and Head of the Department of Architecture and Civic
Planning, University of Nottingham,
President of the Town Planning Institute*

It is usual to look to the United States of America for an antici-
patory glimpse of what may be expected to happen in Britain in
10—15 years' time. Such glimpses have given many warnings of
things to come, whether supermarkets, skyscrapers, spaceships or
subtopias. But in the case of new towns the situation is different.
Here at least Britain can claim to be ahead of the United States
and the continuing programme of new towns in Britain has
become a source of international admiration and even envy.

What is relevant to this country's experience, therefore, is not
the new town concept as such but the example of the role of private
enterprise in new town projects provided by the new town of
Columbia in the United States and the pioneer efforts of Mr
James Rouse in bringing together private capital and private
development agencies to plan and build on a comprehensive scale,
as an alternative to numerous small-scale, unrelated projects for
suburban extensions, or partial urban renewal developments. Mr
Rouse is a real estate developer but is not simply interested in
real estate for its own sake. Quite clearly he is looking beyond
the financial mechanisms and rewards to the end-results and
judges his success by the quality of the environment achieved.

In Britain the idea of new towns was initiated more than a half
century ago by the semi-private non-profit-making organisations
responsible for the establishment of Letchworth and Welwyn.
They pointed the way so successfully that the government, after
the last war, promoted a New Towns Act and sponsored a vigor-
ous programme for the construction of new towns, which now
number 18 in various stages of development, with several more
in the planning stage.

The government has made finance available, provided legislation
for the acquisition of land and set up special development corporations to be responsible for the implementation of the programme.

It has given special concessions putting the development corporations in a most favourable position to get things done on an economic basis. However, resources for public capital investment are always limited, and subject to many calls upon them—and it is understandable that a government wishing to extend its programme of new town building even further may wish to find the means to do so without involving additional public expenditure. Over the past few years the government has, in fact, looked increasingly to the private sector for help in this respect. In the latest batch of new towns it has encouraged private enterprise to undertake the larger proportion of the development of the town centres and to contribute at least 50 per cent of the housing. But if private enterprise is expected to make such a substantial contribution, should we not consider the possibility that private enterprise could be extended to the new town as a whole with those responsible financially brought in at the initial stages of a new town project to participate intelligently and creatively in the whole process of analysis, design and implementation?

Such a conception should not be considered as opposed to the public development corporations, but rather as an extension of activity, a sharing out and a clarification of responsibility, to enable more new towns to be built within a mixed economy. Knowledge in this field is not advanced by taking up sides and I do not, either as an individual or as President of the Town Planning Institute, wish to go on record as supporting either private enterprise against public enterprise, or *vice-versa*. I simply wish—in common with most planners—to see that the right opportunities are given in both sectors for creative planning and to see the case examined for new procedures and a new kind of private development corporation to take on wider responsibilities so that private patronage can be exercised on a nobler scale, with design and social standards built into the initial plans, so avoiding the frustrations which inevitably arise if it is left to the later and wrong stage of the process to examine the plans and introduce statutory development controls.

The public, and more particularly the financial intermediaries—banks, building societies, insurance companies, and development agencies—require projects in which to invest their funds profitably. It is high time that organisational means were found to enable them to do so on the kind of scale on which private enterprise had successfully operated in the past to create an environment of undoubted high quality. They have done so in the past without any need for conferences or town planning legislation—at Bath and Brighton, for example. Today it seems impossible to get anything done without consulting a lot of town planning manuals and going through all sorts of legislative processes. There is a need for a radical simplification of planning procedures to give the freest possible conditions for creative effort.

The aim of this Conference is to provide an opportunity for discussion of these considerations in the light of Mr Rouse's experience with Columbia new town.

JAMES W. ROUSE is president of The Rouse Company, a mortgage banking and real estate development firm with executive offices in Baltimore, Maryland. He was a member of President Eisenhower's Advisory Committee on Housing and chairman of the Sub-committee that recommended the urban renewal programme embraced in the Housing Act of 1954. In 1955 he was engaged by the District of Columbia to lay out a workable programme of urban renewal for the city of Washington. He has lectured on housing, design, and community development at Johns Hopkins, Harvard, and the University of California.

Mr Rouse is an active member of numerous public and private bodies including: vice-chairman, Urban America (formerly president); member of the steering committee of the National Urban Coalition; member of the advisory board of the Federal City Council of Washington; member of the Executive Committee of the Greater Baltimore Committee (formerly chairman); founding member of the Business Committee for the Arts.

II. Columbia: A New Town Built with Private Capital

JAMES ROUSE

President of The Rouse Company

I confess to feeling somewhat uneasy about being present in the role of a novice among 'old pros'. The Columbia venture is only 16 months old, and hardly has the maturity of success and error, and the opportunity of learning from both, that British new towns have had. We in the United States owe Britain much for its early thinking, for the philosophy of Ebenezer Howard, for the early towns and the post-war towns, and for the proof to the world that this in fact was 'do-able' and must be done. It has been a very reassuring and challenging thing to us over the years to see this happening here, while in America we were continuing to follow a trend of disorderly, aimless sprawl in seeking to accommodate the tremendous growth that we face.

Despite our short experience and necessary limitations in the development of Columbia, I feel that a great many question-marks and problems are already behind us. To be sure, a judicious look at the inside of things might indicate that we have more confidence than we deserve, but anyway we have it! But we do realise that there are many open items about which we ourselves are uncertain, and many changes that may have to be made in the planning and development programme. If I seem to fail to give an adequate voice to that uncertainty you can nonetheless be sure it is here. In reporting to you on what we are doing I do not wish to exhort you, certainly not to boast about where we are, but simply to report in the hope that what we are about may be of interest and that perhaps, even, some of it could be useful in your developments here. There is very little about it that we consider secret and there is nothing that we are not happy to disclose to you or are unwilling to be questioned on.

I intend first of all to discuss what I believe to be the most important part of the story: the process in which we have been engaged of bringing forth a plan and a development programme. I genuinely believe this process to be the rightest thing about what we are doing. The same process used by different people in different circumstances could lead to very different results, but I believe that the manner in which we are going about the planning has been a very strengthening thing to us and very convincing to us, that in this process there is real vitality. I will report as a part of this process the progress we have made to date and where we stand in our development schedule.

Secondly, I will endeavour to extract the lessons that have been learned; the meaning so far of what has been attempted.

Prologue to Planning

In the United States we are not really aware of the scale and vigour of our growth as a nation. In America the equivalent of a new town of 350,000 people is built *every month*. We add to our population in every year the equivalent of a Denver, Dallas and San Diego. We will add 6 million to the population of New York region in the next 20 years. Half of the houses that will exist in California by 1988 have not yet been started. This is prodigious growth.

In the last 20 years Baltimore has added a city larger than Houston to its metropolitan area population, and will add a city larger than Kansas City in the next 20 years. In that same period Washington is expected to add a city bigger than Baltimore to its population.

These elements of growth are predictable, yet we operate in our nation as if they are unpredictable. Although the planners and people who look at figures can know the relative scale of growth that we face in our metropolitan areas, it is safe to say that not one single metropolitan area in the United States has comprehensive plans to accommodate this growth that are anything like up to the scale of the minimum standards that we know we should like to see provided. We continue in a disorderly way to add rings of sprawl to our great cities, our middle-size and small cities.

To explain my interest in all this I must say a word or two about the nature of my company. In America a mortgage banker represents the great life insurance companies, the pension funds, the large sources of institutional money, investing their funds in real estate, making investments in local communities. My company is fairly big in this mortgage banking business, with offices across the country in Baltimore, Washington, Pittsburg, Chicago, San Francisco, and soon in Los Angeles. This is how the 'bits and pieces' of a city known as 'sprawl' are financed.

About 12 years ago our entry into the development business followed from the market research and urban studies we had undertaken as background for our mortgage banking business. In the end we were developing major shopping centres on quite a large scale—regional centres with two, three or four department stores and 50 to 200 shops between the stores. These were large projects costing many millions of dollars. They were really *new town centres* but they had not been fully recognised as such in America.

Out of these two businesses we have seen the void, the deficit, the fractured growth, and we have also from time to time seen the tremendously strong interaction that occurs when the elements of growth are brought in relationship to one another in an orderly way. When stores, offices, houses and apartments, open spaces, can be better organised, better values are created; commerce runs better; better living is provided for people. As we began seeing this (both from the standpoint of the public or extra-curricula duties in which all of us in business tend to be involved—planning boards, committees, and so on—looking at the public demand for a better answer, and from the business standpoint looking at the private profit opportunities for doing this better) we in the company kept asking ourselves the questions, 'Could not we really put all these things together in one new city? Would it be possible for us to assemble enough land to build not a sub-division, not a large regional shopping centre, but a city? And what would the economics of doing it be? Would it be profitable to engage in it? Could a private developer make an approach to city building that showed greater respect for what I will call the dignity of the land itself and of man himself, by arranging those things in a more orderly and felicitous way that are going to happen anyway? Would it be profitable to do this?' As we kept talking of this in our own organisation we finally concluded that we should make a hypothetical run of what it would be like to build a city.

We felt that a city of 100,000 people was about the minimum size that would provide sufficient markets to give the variety, choice and opportunities—the full fabric of life—that a person would seek and want and be well served by in an urban environment. It was a fairly arbitrary choice but it seemed then (as now) to have been a fairly rational one.

We then broke down the components of a city of 100,000 people, going to Racine, Wisconsin, midway between Chicago and Milwaukee, dissecting it in terms of all the things that happened in Racine: the number of filling stations, YMCAs, libraries, churches, the income level of the people, the kind of housing, and the whole fabric of the city. A kind of check list of what people did, what it was they had brought forth over 125 years, was laid out. Then, taking Charlotte, a city of 200,000 people in North Carolina, with no big city nearby, a similar thing was done to see if the same sort of inventory was derived. From this, and from subjective judgements about what should happen in the way of open space within a framework of an urban environment, the conclusion was reached that it would take 12,000 acres of land to produce this city of 100,000 people with the amenities it was sought to provide.

We then went through a whole economic model based on acquiring that land, improving it with utilities and streets, financing it, marketing it, and carrying the process forward year by year. How would it work out economically? Would it be profitable to develop this city and sell all the land? Our role as a developer of buildings was ignored, the feeling being that it was collateral to this exercise. We had to look upon the whole thing as if we were to develop it and sell all the land. Was it profitable to do it? Our estimates suggested that not only would it be extremely profitable to engage in such an operation; *it appeared to be more profitable to build a good environment than a bad one.*

The next step was to focus on an area between Baltimore and Washington of some 30,000 acres, and to draw a ring around it to show that we would be satisfied to build anywhere within it. Our choice of site for the development of Columbia was influenced by its position—23 miles from Washington and 17 miles from Baltimore—by the new 8-lane expressway between the two cities, by the existence of Friendship Airport, and by its characteristic beautiful rolling farm land with many wonderful woods and small ponds and streams and lovely old lanes that we have since preserved and incorporated in the neighbourhood structure wherever possible.

[16]

Having settled on a site, a few farms were bought to establish some indication of market price. We then came face to face with 'the American dilemma'. Despite the fact that the city building business is the largest single industry in the country (by 'city building' I do not of course mean building cities at one time but the process of building houses, apartments, stores and offices), there was no one single large corporation engaged in it; it was a proliferation of little enterprises and there was not in America a single developer with the scale of resources needed to go out and acquire the land on which to build a city. Although the big industrial giants could have done it out of their vest pocket, for any real estate developer it was a gigantic financial task beyond his capacity. So, armed with our hypothesis and an economic model, our sampling of the land, our map and a statement seeking to prove why this was enormously in the public interest as well as prospectively profitable, we went to the traditional sources of capital in the city building business—the great life insurance companies. We sat down with the Chairman of the Board of the Connecticut General Life Insurance Company and laid out before him and his people this opportunity.

What sort of approach was made? We went to the Connecticut General seeking an entirely different relationship from the customary one—not a two-thirds loan or a 70 per cent loan but all the money needed to do the job, because it could not be done by a bootstrap or with the deadline of an interest payment or maturity date breathing down our necks. We had to be able to approach this project with sure funds available. This was the only way in which to create the superior environment which was an essential part of the economic aspect. The Insurance Company were therefore asked to put up all the money involved and to share the venture 50–50. They were unlikely to lose money because a large acreage of land was being acquired between two great cities. There was risk; but we regarded it as minimal, and it was the Insurance Company's opportunity to make a profit and to contribute in a significant way to an important national venture.

The Connecticut General agreed. It was the largest single investment in the history of the Company: $23\frac{1}{2}$ million were committed to the purchase of land. The money was provided with the freedom to move as was seen fit within this 30,000-acre area. The commitment to finance was obtained in February 1963, and we then started acquiring the land. There were three years in which to buy the land but we soon discovered that unless we moved swiftly the pressure of our activity would, over time, escalate prices out of reach. Nine months later 14,000 acres of land had been purchased, some 145 separate farms and parcels. It was a contiguous land area that allowed us to be identified for the first time as the purchaser. Until then there had been an increasing awareness that there was some intensive activity with respect to land going on in the county, but nobody knew who it was or for what purpose. Rumours and anxieties were tumbling through the area. In October of 1963 we walked into the office of the County Commissioners of Howard County and identified ourselves as the buyers of 10 per cent of their county. It was a traumatic moment for them! This is a county of 55,000 people and we had acquired what looked like a piece of Swiss cheese, the holes in the cheese comprising some 13 existing sub-divisions where lived 7,500 people. Our land was all in and around and through this area. We had acquired enough land so we knew that we could run our sewer and water lines and roads without seeking any governmental condemnation powers or any special rights or privileges.

Many of the county's voters lived in the middle of this land area and in 1962 the County Commissioners had been elected to public office in a 'revolution' in the community. They were Republican and had overthrown the Democrats for the first time in 40 years. The central issue in the election campaign had been zoning, with the Republicans out to defend the county against urbanisation and to preserve low density development. They had accused the Democrats of having sold out to the home builders and generally of violating the bucolic charm of the county. So here we were, one year later, saying that we had bought 10 per cent of the county and wanted to build a city! This was really a horrendous political dilemma for the County Commissioners.

The Planning Process

We faced the dilemma confronting all development in America: the problem of winning the planning and zoning approval necessary to do what we wanted to do. We were completely at the

[18]

mercy of the county government and so of the people of the county. We had no votes, no influence, no control. This was very useful really, for the following week, at a public meeting with the people of the county, who had chips a foot high on their shoulders about what was happening, we could honestly state that they held all the cards! They had nothing to fear. We were the only people who had to be afraid: we had invested at that point 20 million dollars in the purchase of land which we could not possibly develop without major changes in zoning, therefore we had to produce in the following year a plan which was a so much better solution to what they could see was otherwise going to occur that they would buy it and we would win zoning, or, if we failed in that, we would lose zoning. We were the people to be concerned, not they. We were able to say that we would spend a year in planning. (They could not believe we did not already have plans but we did not.) We said that after a year we would come back and present our plans to the county and seek the zoning permission necessary to fulfil the plans. *Our land was at that time zoned for half- or one-acre lots or even as farmhouses.*

We began our planning in the fall of 1963 and continued it through 1964. We went back in the fall of 1964 and presented our plans to the county. We made a tabloid size presentation which we mailed to every resident. We set up a display and wrote to all of the residents anywhere in our area, some 20,000 people, and said we would meet with them from 10 a.m. till 10 p.m. seven days a week in groups of one to 100 to discuss the impact of the plan on their property, to share with them in it, and to revise it if necessary, before we requested any change in zoning.

What we were negotiating for entailed an entirely new approach to zoning. This county, like most urban counties in the United States, had fixed zoning classifications, a very rigid envelope placed around a legally identifiable piece of land. We proposed an entirely new kind of zoning, called 'New Town District Zoning', with basic criteria that would have to be met on overall densities, quantities of land in open space, broad indications of low-density, medium-density and high-density housing, broad indications of neighbourhood centres, village centres, downtown, indications of employment centres (the phrase used to describe all the various classifications of business and industry), and a whole new process by which zoning would be granted. We sought to have this new zoning classification established and then to have our land zoned accordingly.

The politicians faced a real problem. If they consented to our zoning proposal they might be accused of 'rolling over and playing dead' to a big developer who had come into the county, yet it was obvious that there was gathering support in the county for Columbia.

A young lawyer who was counsel for the County Commissioners brought things to a head when he declared the whole zoning proposal unconstitutional and unlawful and thereby seemed to have killed it. This proved to be a fortuitous step from our standpoint. For the first time we were the underdog, and we were able to see whether people really did care about this. Sure enough, they did: one by one various organisations began passing resolutions supporting Columbia. The local newspaper ran a poll on its front page—asking readers whether they were for or against Columbia, and week by week reported the state of opinion. The percentage for Columbia kept rising. In the end the Company's proposals were declared to have been revised sufficiently to be legally acceptable, so we were then ready for the public hearings and the full process that would follow.

The zoning hearing was then set up, to go from noon to midnight. A very short time was needed to present the Company's case as it had already been so extensively presented through the county. The opposition were then called, and in this county of 55,000 people not one single person opposed the zoning. The zoning was granted in the summer of 1965 and it was then possible to begin serious engineering and to conduct tests.

Having got the required zoning, we then faced a whole new financing schedule. We had to go back to the Connecticut General Life Insurance Company to say that we now had the land and zoning and were ready, in accordance with the original deal, to propose a system for financing the full development. We proposed a new financing of $50 million which was to include the land purchase and our estimate of the cash funds required to move forward with development. We then built a new economic model and estimated every single item of expenditure year by year through to completion: every foot of sewer, water, roads, every dollar of interest, of taxes and insurance, the administrative and the marketing costs, advertising, sales, concrete, bricks and mortar; and then the pace of development and the income from the sale of land.

Obviously the money going into land development investment was far larger in the early years than the proceeds from land sales, so debt outstanding would build up gradually to some $50 million. What the Company sought was the funds to cover that entire gap between cost and proceeds from land sales. It was therefore proposed that the Connecticut General should accept half of this $50 million investment and that other investors be found to take the other half. This plan was accepted and the Connecticut General was joined by the Teachers Insurance and Annuity Association and the Chase Manhattan Bank. In this way the money was obtained, with four years to draw it down and ten in which to pay it back, all of which was comfortably within the limits of the economic model.

In June 1966 we broke ground for the first time. In July 1967 the first family moved into Columbia. Now, some 16 months later, there are something over 2,000 people living there. Eight hundred families have bought houses or apartments. We have created about 3,000 jobs. The city is well under way. We will add more than 3,000 dwelling units in the next 12 months and more than 10,000 people, and a year from today we will have a population of between 12,000 and 15,000. We should grow at the rate of about 10,000 people a year to completion by 1980. Then, or shortly thereafter, Columbia should be a city of about 125,000 people.

Planning Goals and Implementation

The planning process began in the fall of 1963 with a set of goals to discipline the venture. The first goal was that we should build an entire city. The studies which we had made provided statistical data on the activities of people in a city of 100,000. We added to that a great deal by way of our own knowledge and concern about the things we felt should happen: about the schools and churches, libraries and colleges, hospitals, concert halls, restaurants, hotels, stores, apartment houses. We wanted to provide a full residential, educational, cultural, recreational and vocational life within the city. There should be as many jobs in the city as there were dwelling units. It should be possible for anyone to work and live

[21]

there, whether he was a janitor or a corporation executive. These were the ingredients of the city as we defined it for ourselves.

Secondly, the plan should respect the land. The basic topography was carefully recorded, the location of streams, valleys, forests; the old buildings, which were to be preserved; the tree-lined roads; all the things which ought to be left as they were. Through these 'overlays', the land imposed its own disciplines on the planning process.

Thirdly, along with these activities we undertook what from our standpoint was the most important exercise of all and what, strangely enough, seems to be the most unique effort in which we engaged (although one might think it would be the elementary starting point of all town planning): we began by saying that developers, planners, architects, engineers, bankers, are not the most competent people to fashion life in a city, are not the people with the best knowledge of the way people can live with other people most effectively. We have an enormously 'examined' society in which ministers, doctors, psychiatrists, psychologists, social scientists, have learned a lot about people's ability to live together in an urban environment. Yet this knowledge seems to parade down one side of the street and the development professions down the other, with virtually no dialogue between, so that the essential experience which should motivate planning and design and development practice is unused.

So we brought together a group of 14 people chosen largely from the behavioural sciences. We took those areas of knowledge in which we felt we needed special help—education, health, community relationship, religion—and then tried to find people who seemed to be informed, open, objective, wise, in these areas. We called dozens of people around the United States whose opinion we respected. We would list the input we wanted and ask for recommendations, and, as recommendations seemed to focus then on sets of names, those were the names we went after. It is interesting that nobody we called refused to participate; everyone we sought came. We wound up with the Head of Psychiatry in the School of Public Health at Johns Hopkins; a Professor of Psychology from the University of Michigan, who is a perceptive, knowledgeable man in the field of communications; a young writer/student/reporter in the field of education who seemed to know all the biases; the City Manager from Oakland, California, who was the most imaginative City Manager in America; the Commissioner of Recreation of the City of Philadelphia, a remarkable woman; a sociologist with the General Electric Company who was Director of Consumer Behaviour Research—and others, 14 in all. We asked this group of people, drawn from multiple disciplines, to come and meet with us. Every two weeks for five months we met on Thursday night for dinner, and all day Friday and all day Saturday. Our injunctions were very simple. We said: 'We have not brought you together to plan a Utopia. We must make the decisions. We are the developer. We cannot relinquish the responsibility for that. We do not seek your recommendations. We do not want any reports. We want conversation in depth about the optima that we can define in our society. What is the finest possible educational system that we can conceive in a city of 100,000 people? Forget whether it is feasible or not. Let us explore the best that we know in education, in health, in communications. How can religion be most effective? What about loneliness and delinquency? What about the college-educated housewife with two children and little fulfilment? How do these sources of irritation, of frustration, of unfulfilment, arise? What does all this say to us, after we have engaged in it, as developers, as planners? How does it speak out to us in the manner that the land speaks out to us in the laying out of a plan?

We decided to seek this understanding first to help us plan and secondly to inform us, so that as developers we could be better equipped to deal with the institutions and processes in the community and to work in the fields of education, health, communications, welfare, recreation, in ways that would be constructive and bring forth the best and most valid relationships. We believed the honest, fundamental purpose of a city must be to produce a better civilisation: that it was possible to produce a constructive environment for the growth of people. This was the product we were trying to produce and we felt sure that if we could do this it would be more profitable; that the public interest and private profit purposes were precisely compatible here; that if we were able to show a better environment, so would people want to live there, so would businesses want to locate there, and so would the community prosper. Instead of conflict which our society finds so often in these motivations, we sought a compatibility of purposes that had not previously been tied together

[23]

in the productive way that a free society and a free market ought to be able to achieve.

Our fourth goal in the planning process was to make a profit. We will regard Columbia as a failure if it does not make an enormous profit; if we have not proved by the end of the job that it is so much more profitable to build a good city than a bad one then people will not stop building bad ones. We want to prove that we can draw the development business into a new approach to city building, and we will—if we are as right as we hope and believe we are. In looking at land and at environment and the wholeness of a city in this way, we found that the profit objective was not suffocating the planning process but invigorating it, a fact which was brought home to the planners and sociologists too.

Ours was a democratic process of planning, for *we always had to try to take the voting of the market into consideration in relation to our planning*. The temptation of architects or planners or developers is to impose their own bias, their own aspiration, assuming that they know what people ought to want, but this kind of arrogance is brought down to reality by a continuing examination of market voting.

The market had an invigorating effect in other ways. Our product was environment and it had to be good. Amenities matter because they produce value. If we could not offer a superior range of amenities in open space, recreation, community facilities, variety of life and choice, a city fabric that was much more vital and real than alternative offerings, then the market would condemn us. Therefore this 'market look' was continually vitalising the pre-servicing of the community and the range of amenities that we were to offer.

By the fall of 1964 this process was finished and a plan produced that was offered to the community. It had no 'skyrocket' innovations. If it had merit, it was the product of good craftsmanship rather than ingenious new solutions. I think we found, as many of us would, that we actually know a lot about life if we take the trouble to marshal our knowledge. Good environment implies a simpler set of conditions than we are apt to realise.

Some very clear principles emerged to influence the shaping of the plan. At the beginning of the group sessions there had been a strong bias towards a highly sophisticated urbanity; but as the

[24]

group came to examine the questions of people living with people, how a health system might work, how an educational system could best work, communications among people, matters of environment, they came to believe more and more that scale mattered enormously; that there are levels of community that need to be recognised, and that as they are recognised things begin to fall together with remarkable overlap between the number of people who are best served in terms of health, education, recreation, supermarkets, and so on. Our planning came to emphasise the creation of 'place' at every opportunity. For example, what we came to call the neighbourhood was planned around an elementary school. The school system became fundamental to the development of the plan. After great discussion back and forth we reached the conclusion that there was no doubt among any of us that we would plump for small schools and not big schools; schools in which there were more winners and fewer losers; schools in which there were more team captains, more debaters, more people in the drama club, more opportunity for the individual child to be noticed by the teachers and staff; more opportunity for relationships between teacher, parent and child; more opportunity for each of these functions in life to be a part of the community rather than functions separate from the community. So the elementary school became almost the beginning of planning in the neighbourhood, with schools of 600 to 700 in neighbourhoods of 700 to 1,000 dwellings.

Related to the school was the need to bring together everything that could function at this neighbourhood level: a child care centre for the two- to five-year olds; a small store; a swimming pool; a playground; meeting rooms. These formed a neighbourhood centre. All dwelling units in that neighbourhood reached the neighbourhood centre by a path system separate from the road system. A group of such neighbourhoods comprising a population of 10,000 to 15,000 became a village, and at the village centre again we tried to marshal the maximum opportunity for 'place'. At the village centre was the high school and middle school of 800 to 1,000 children each. Although more and more American high schools and middle schools have become consolidated schools serving large areas, in Columbia they have been planned as community schools, placed at the heart of every village, together with a youth centre, a year-round swimming pool, tennis courts, supermarkets and 15 to 20 other stores selling convenience goods and services, a bank, a beauty parlour, churches, a library, a small quantity of offices, meeting rooms, places for arts, crafts, music—all the things that would be needed by this population of 10,000 to 15,000 people.

The idea of 'place' in the neighbourhood and villages means that people will come together voluntarily, unself-consciously, in the normal process of life, meet one another, know one another, share problems and fears and opportunities. Teacher, minister, doctor, merchant, parent and child will come in contact through the natural process of living, able to share yearnings and problems. This is not the creation of a regimented society but of a free society with a much wider range of choices and opportunities to implement those choices.

The villages are connected to one another and separated from one another by an open space system. Of the 14,000 acres comprising Columbia, 3,200 acres are committed to permanent open space which interlaces the whole city. Each village centre—nine in all—is connected by a bus system, with its own right of way, that also runs to downtown. Eventually 40 per cent of the housing will be within three minutes walk of a bus-stop. Town roads are little junior freeways only entered by neighbourhood roads. There is no parking access into the village centre: all parking is around the stores and at the back.

Downtown is very big, the place where all the big things should be—the department stores, the major office buildings, the hotels, restaurants, theatres, college, hospital, a big park, a lake, a symphony pavilion. These are all brought together in a downtown that will be very big and very lively, designed to serve in practice a larger area than a city of 125,000 people. In the circumstances of Columbia it is probable that it will.

Industry is planned at various locations through the city appropriate to its needs. Some forms of industry care about expressway location. The clean, campus-type industry needs to be well served in other respects. Warehousing, distribution and light manufacturing want low-cost land and different kinds of facilities. Different kinds of industrial locations are therefore provided. All commercial zoning has been eliminated in Columbia and reduced to parkland. This has been made possible by spreading the cost of open space over the entire project.

[26]

We have about 125 people working full-time on our staff in Columbia. They include people engaged in market research, assembly of data on individual market problems relating to housing, business and industry. There is a very large planning and design staff.

There are also an engineering department concerned with land development, a marketing and sales department to market the land and a subsidiary development corporation developing apartments, shopping centres, office buildings and industrial buildings. (Our policy is to sell all the land to home builders, now about 16 in number and between them producing over 60 individual sample houses, as well as apartments.)

We have deliberately allowed a wide variety of taste from colonial to contemporary design. We did not want to produce a community which seemed to have been imprinted. All houses have to go through an Architectural Review Committee where everybody disagrees with them as either too precious or too vulgar! Its role is an unhappy one, but in general it tries to sift out the gross and the tasteless while allowing the individual to build what he wants provided he stays within reasonable limits. Some areas have been designated as 'high visibility' areas, and there is much more strict control in these.

We also have an institutional planning and development division concerned entirely with schools, colleges, hospitals, churches and all the institutional aspects of the community. Success in building a city of this sort depends absolutely on the fabric of the whole. A wide range of markets must be identified and all approached simultaneously. Building cannot be done in series; it must be parallel. We cannot bring people first and then provide swimming pools and stores. We have to sell the credibility of the whole exercise. We now have two department stores and 50 other shops providing over half-a-million square feet of retail floor space that will open in 1970 in downtown Columbia, with only 2,000 people now living there. We have an office building of 100,000 square feet under construction (having just finished one of 50,000 square feet). It is financed 100 per cent by the Equitable Life Assurance Society of New York and up to now there is not one single tenant. We have to believe—we know—that the tenants will come. We have hundreds of acres of land laid out for industry and now 15 industries are committed. Seven different industries have committed to Columbia in one of each of the last seven weeks. We signed a 30-year contract with the National Symphony to make Columbia its summer home before there was a single person there. We have to move in all these markets at the same time—housing, stores, industry, hospitals, libraries, schools and community facilities—and they all interact favourably. It is this interconnection that creates a city.

The official opening was 14 July, 1967. We had not expected that the first thing to open in Columbia would be a music pavilion in the park adjacent to downtown, but by the grace of God this was what occurred. The first performance of the National Symphony with Van Cliburn as soloist took place at Columbia on 15 July in the midst of the worst downpour imaginable! Last summer there were no less than 54 events in the pavilion, ranging from the New York City Ballet to rock-and-roll.

Since then, in the development of Columbia to date, all the streets and utilities for four neighbourhoods have been completed. We now have four neighbourhood centres and the first village centre. There are five swimming pools, a community centre at the heart of the village with a stage, kitchen and facilities for anything from church in the morning to theatre at night. There are three other meeting rooms in the village centre, a year-round swimming pool, tennis courts, two golf courses, riding stables, hunting preserve. A bus system is operating and there is a variety of housing, for sale or rent, both low price and moderate rent and high price and rent. Some 350 apartments and 500 houses have been finished; 20 stores; 50,000 square feet of offices; there are four industries now operating and 13 more to come. The first two department stores are committed. It is the beginning of a city, and it says so to anyone arriving at Columbia.

Lessons Learned

The lessons learned are important. We have learned that it is possible to assemble land on a large scale, to zone it and finance it. We have found that our institutions are enormously ready to respond to this new kind of opportunity. A new educational system is emerging. The first elementary school has open classrooms,

[28]

with team teaching, ungraded. The focus is on developing the individual child's desire to learn rather than the teacher's desire to teach. The response of the churches has been extraordinary; 13 major Protestant denominations have joined together to form a Religious Facilities Corporation. The Catholic Archdiocese has joined, and the Jews. The Catholics, Protestants and Jews now have a single Religious Facilities Corporation owning all their church buildings. This is more than just ownership of buildings; it is the beginning of co-operative community action. The Corcoran School of Art has opened classes and the Peabody Conservatory of Music has classes for music and ballet. The Symphony is there, and Howard County Community College will be built adjacent to downtown. There will be the Dag Hammerschold College, with 60 per cent of its students and faculty from overseas, built adjacent to downtown.

Even in this early stage, the attempt to produce a better environment has shown itself to be a marketable product among home buyers and tenants and among people in business and industry. It is evident that in the Columbia environment merchants will do more business, people in the offices will hold their employees longer, industry will be attracted, and altogether it will provide a much better way of life for the people. There has been a tremendous response in the institutions of American society to this opportunity to provide a better community.

All the indications are that we are going to be able to prove that it is more profitable to provide a good environment than a bad one, and that is the most important lesson we can show.

Some Questions and Answers
on the Columbia Experiment

Question: Does the city of Columbia cater mainly for middle- and high-income bracket families? Have the sociologists pressed for the inclusion of some form of cheaper housing?

Answer: The premise is incorrect. Housing will be offered at rents and prices well within the range of the lower-middle market. The unskilled labourer making in America 2 dollars an hour for 40 hours a week is regarded as a kind of base peg for this purpose. There will be apartments for rent in Columbia at rents he can afford.

Where there is more than one person working in a family (which is often the case in the lower income levels) rents will be accessible to people with wages as low as 3,000 or 4,000 dollars a year.

An illustration is the case of a woman living in a ghetto in Baltimore with her six-year-old child. She rented an apartment (living room, bedroom, kitchen, dining room, and all utilities paid for) in Columbia at less than the 30 dollars a week she was paying for two rooms in the ghetto. She then moved into the apartment in Columbia with her child and obtained employment as a maid, for an employer living only a block away.

The 14,500-dollar house, at 136 dollars a month, is within the buying capacity of almost any skilled worker in America. I agree we will not immediately reach the indigent. We shall surely create our own indigent over time, and we will have to find out how to provide for them. We hope our society will have sufficient concern to discover ways to do it. But I really believe that we shall be well able to fulfil our primary purpose, which is that anyone who works in Columbia will be able to find housing at rents or prices appropriate to his wages.

Q. What is the policy in Columbia with regard to coloured people?

A. Our position has been made clear from the beginning—that this was to be an inter-racial community—even before zoning was obtained and during the period when we needed to win friends in this county which had voted for Wallace in the Democratic Primary in 1964, and where the general disposition of the people was fairly clear. During the period of planning and prior to zoning we never flinched from the question of colour and always insisted that this was to be a fully open community.

[30]

It was interesting that this was never used against us; that people seemed willing to accept the prospect of an inter-racial community in Columbia whereas they would have been terrified by a development next door to them. The ability to see the community within the scale of an entire city made them willing to accept apartments and town houses and all kinds of physical manifestations which they would probably have abhorred had it been presented in pieces. In the same way they were willing to accept a fully open community. When we launched the marketing of Columbia we did those things which must be done by people who mean what they say about colour. In our exhibit building we had photographs of black and white children in the school and in the swimming pools and in the community. We had black as well as white receptionists. The result was that there has never been any question that Columbia is fully open. There is no apartment house and no neighbourhood that does not have black as well as white people. It is the most racially unself-conscious community I have ever seen. It is amazing that this has happened midway between Baltimore and Washington, where racial pressures are enormous with Washington today almost 60 per cent and Baltimore 40 per cent black. At the first election in the community held to elect a board of directors for The Village of Wild Lake Board, one of the five directors elected was a negro. This was not done by the community out of any sense of guilt, pride or self-consciousness. They had not even been there long enough to achieve any of these conditions. This was a good man and he was elected. That was all there was to it. It has been a very encouraging experience.

Q. Is there any policy in Columbia with regard to mobile homes?

A. No. We have not done anything in this respect. I do not think we will—at least in their present form. There are some great possibilities in this field that have yet to be properly explored: for example, in the manufacturing of housing components the prospects could be immense if the point was reached where a person could buy a manufactured kitchen, bathroom, living room and bedroom and hitch them together in various combinations; but the mobile home in its present shape has not appealed to us as a really satisfactory system.

Q. The whole motive of new towns in Britain has been to build living conditions for a cross-section of the community, including homes for low-income families, a large number of whom could not possibly afford the

[31]

kind of homes being marketed in Columbia. Until people can afford these things for themselves, does not housing have to be regarded to some extent as a social service, with those who can afford to pay paying more and those who could not paying less? Should not private enterprise be harnessed to the task of seeking to house the whole population rather than be allowed simply to 'cream off' the profitable bits?

Secondly, does not American differ from British experience in that in Britain it might be considered more desirable, where open space between two cities was scarce, to preserve it as a place of recreation rather than allow it to be used for profitable private development?

A. The second question underscores what I would also say in answer to the first. There is a dreadful tendency, in looking at the urban problem, to over-simplify the problem and over-complicate the answer. We seek to test what might be a legitimate truth in respect of the urban problem by measuring it against the entire urban problem. But if it fails to solve the entire urban problem it should not be pronounced insufficient. Not one of the 20 or so new towns in Britain is going significantly to solve the problem of urban slums; but that does not make the new towns unimportant. They make a major contribution in their own right.

The question underlines the total complication of an urban society. By what process are these decisions to be made? We only really make them as we begin to approach the whole growth of the nation. I speak of the United States because I do not know England well enough to philosophise. Columbia is, I believe, a very important answer, but to try to find in it the answer to the Washington ghetto would be ridiculous and I would not attempt to do so. But that does not make Columbia unimportant. Similarly, if the new towns in Britain account for 150,000 dwelling units and some 3 million dwelling units have been built by private enterprise, I would wonder what 'drain off' is occurring through that process. Perhaps part of the 3 million units to be built over the next period of time could be marshalled into a better solution than is provided at present by inadequately-planned development of those 3 million dwelling units. Could not just a part of it provide a comprehensive new community, though it might not deal as directly with the problem of the London ghetto as a government new town? In this way it may be possible to reach some other very important answers. Even higher standards may be set for other new towns; or ways may be found of marshalling that part of the private market to reach deeper down than had hitherto been possible. There are all kinds of things that might stem from action of this sort.

Certainly, Columbia has not answered the problem of the Washington ghetto. Nonetheless, within the range of its 125,000 people, it will say some very important things about the Washington/Baltimore ghettoes. There are bound to be some who will move to Columbia. Others who have moved out of the ghetto only eight or ten years ago into better income jobs will in turn find in Columbia a way of life they never dreamed of knowing as black people in American society. In Columbia planning has been approached first in terms of systems of education and health and communication and community, and then residually in terms of physical planning, in the belief that through this process one arrives at a better plan and a better profit.

I believe that this same process is also the way in which to deal with the ghetto in Washington and in Baltimore. To that end we have set up another corporation called the American City Corporation in which we are enlisting talent, believing that we can put ourselves to work on the problem of the old city by applying the same basic processes that we have applied in Columbia. There are things we have learned in those processes that we can put to work in an old city. We can go out into the heart of the ghetto and find the family, impoverished and inadequately educated and in poor health, asking questions about how that family becomes educable, healthy, joyful, with neighbours who care about it. What kind of environment or institutions will it take to do that? What kind of new processes of education? What kind of health requirements? What kind of jobs? What kind of transportation? What kind of community is needed? What are the answers to these questions? When we find them we can derive processes of planning, housing, transportation, taxation, economics, and come to grips with the problem of the ghetto far more effectively than we do now in the United States by simply dealing with the symptoms of bad housing—crime, drugs, unemployment. That is like sticking a finger in a dyke to shore up a city that does not work.

This is the way in which to tackle the problem of the ghetto. But it would be arrogant to suggest that Columbia could pick up a part of the ghetto and move it. This is not our task. There are many other things to be done about the ghetto than that. But Columbia is an attempt to solve one part of the urban problem and has an importance of its own in that respect.

Q. The image of private enterprise in Britain in the past has been that of only wanting to do the profitable things and not taking responsibility for the unprofitable. In the light of the suggested relationship between good

*design and larger profits, were all the unprofitable things in a new town
like Columbia encompassed? Did the public authority make any contribution at all? Were the Company really taking over the whole responsibility?
Who was responsible for maintenance? How were they managing to do all
the things which in Britain seemed to have to be passed over to the local
authority and paid for out of rates and taxes? Did not the unprofitable
obligations placed on new towns in Britain (to take people from the old
areas and re-house them) vitiate comparisons with Columbia?*

A. I am sure that there is a large area of responsibility that must be
assumed by society, either here or in the United States, that is uneconomic, and therefore beyond the capacity of private enterprise. The
new town approach in Britain is an assumption of part of that burden.
I cannot offer the solution that all the social problems could be answered
economically, but I believe there is a burden on society to use the
market system to its maximum potential in order to shrink the residual
that had to be done by public action. There is a need to create more
dynamic opportunity for the market system.

I have been asked a lot of questions on how we have been able to
provide amenities not provided by the typical individual private
developer. A man with 1,000 acres cannot provide a bus system or
build lakes or extend a public sewer for seven miles. He cannot build
four-lane freeways. He cannot put in 6,000 trees. He cannot do these
things because he does not have a large enough land area against which
to lay off these land improvements. He cannot distribute the burden
and is therefore limited in the things he can do within 100, 500 or 1,000
acres. His objectives must therefore be limited. Simply, the ability to
acquire a large enough land area and to plan over a large enough area
has permitted us to do things which would be totally uneconomic in a
smaller area. It would never have been possible to wipe out the commercial nuisance or to build 800 acres of lakes or to provide community
facilities of the sort provided at Columbia. Because of the sheer scale
of operations we are able to provide a larger number of amenities and
also to offer land at different prices.

This pricing problem was of course a very real one. On what basis
should land be priced when such a huge area was owned? It could not
just be priced at what the market would bring because this would be
the highest price. Arbitrary decisions had to be made to price it in
relation to the desired objective, so that it would fit into the whole
model. In general we have adopted a system of pricing land at 10 times
the monthly rent that a rental project sought to achieve, so that with a
rental of 100 dollars a month the land would be 1,000 dollars a unit.

[34]

All this has to be fitted into the fabric of an economic model. It works because it provides housing for workers. The 3,000-dollar land is just as important to the community because it provides housing for executives. The profit is made not out of the 3,000-dollar land but out of the whole effort being made. This is the kind of economics that only began to work when there was planning and development over a large enough land area.

I cannot really see that the new town will replace private enterprise. There are social responsibilities that society has imposed upon the new town programme in Britain. But it should be possible to use private enterprise much more effectively in using many more markets and in providing much higher quality development, if the right circumstances were given in which it would work most effectively.

Q. The city of Columbia appears to have been planned for 1.8 cars per household yet 60 per cent of the people are within three minutes walk of public transport, which is segregated on separate roads. Did the Columbia team recommend any optimum division between public and private transport for the city, and was the minibus provided as a social service?

A. The whole question of public transportation has been one of the most uncomfortable and uneasy to come before us. We have felt the need for both better knowledge and better technical capacity in the field of public transportation than is now available, and our approach to public transportation has been pragmatic—to try to do something that could work now but that held out the maximum options for things we believe ought to lie ahead with minimal advances in engineering and technology. Therefore we planned our minibus system from an engineering standpoint to be economically self-sustaining over six or seven years, but we did not think it adequate for the future and believe that some kind of automated system would be better. The provision of the separate right of way seemed to us to hold open those options fairly well. We are now engaged on a joint research study to test out the concepts which may lie ahead.

There is, we believe, a social aspect of urban transportation. Those who find our approach to neighbourhood planning primitive or obsolete would perhaps be equally unimpressed with our human concern in dealing with transportation. We saw transportation as a potential meeting place and we plumped for small buses. It enables them to have women as part-time drivers and provides the maximum opportunity for communication. Our studies showed that little buses were

[35]

better in this respect despite the sacrifice of economies of scale from bigger buses. We should like to achieve some form of automated transportation that would be fun to ride in and add joy to people's lives, rather than being just a way of moving about. We hope that this will ultimately be achievable. We are not very comfortable with the present solution, which is part of a continuing search. But, even while providing a public transportation system, we have refused to compromise on the question of adequate choice for people in an automobile society. We are not prepared to say that the provision of public transport is necessarily going to reduce the need for parking spaces. Of course, if this proves to be so, other uses will be found for such land. Admittedly there is now over-provision for parking in town centres and so on, but we feel this is a better risk than forcing people into public transport by making it inconvenient to park. We have elected to make it convenient both to park and to use public transportation: we will resolve any problem of excess land when it arises.

Q. The problem of integrating private enterprises and public services appears to be fundamental. A situation in which private enterprise can work with government to promote better urban design seems quite feasible provided that proper incentive systems can be developed, such as a delaying tax on land, which would permit, say, a large department store or a new town centre development to forego or postpone payment of taxes until its full earning capacity has been reached. Did the Columbia enterprise make any arrangements of this sort with the County?

A. I agree that is a fundamental question. I deplore attempts to separate private enterprise new towns and public new towns as mutually exclusive. There is now a good deal of support for setting up local community corporations. I would agree with this first, because I do not believe it possible for private developers such as our company to develop at the pace that is required in America to meet all growth; second, I think there are situations and circumstances outside many cities that can only be met by public action; third, I think that a local community should be able to form its own development corporation if it wishes.

It seems apparent to me that there are two distinct processes involved in urban development that are not always sufficiently distinguished. One is land development and the other is the development of buildings on the land. The development of the land is I think essentially a public action and I believe that most of the things that we are doing in this respect in Columbia could be done by a local community corporation. In our own book-keeping and in our own management we keep entirely separate the functions of land development and disposition and the development of buildings above ground. The latter activity has to buy land from the land development company and pay an economic price for it. Looked at in this way it is possible to envisage some form of community development corporation assembling land, using compulsory purchase powers denied private developers which enable it to overcome specific points of resistance where necessary, extending the main water and sewage utilities, putting in the roads and providing for open spaces, building the amenities, and incorporating all these amenities in the basic land price. It then markets the land, specifically using private enterprise to subsidise the uneconomic aspects by obtaining a higher price for the land enhanced by these amenities. They are thus billed into the whole economic model.

From what I have seen in Great Britain the government development of retail facilities in new town centres is not realising anything like the full potential of the market that is there in the new towns. The release of this land under competitive circumstances—to people who will bring in the department stores and the shops—would produce a higher price for the land, a higher quality of town centre development and lower prices for the consumer. I think this could be equally true of many aspects of the housing market, and the industrial market. The money made in this way would go to offset deficits for open space or low price land for publicly-subsidised housing. I cannot believe that it is right to think of these two aspects of society, the public role and the private role, as being at loggerheads. Great Britain as a society needs to find the way to use both ventures, both capabilities—the most creative potential that it possibly can—to deal with its problems.

III. Planning
W. A. WEST

Professor of Law relating to Land, College of Estate Management
(University of Reading)

When we speak of planning, we tend to think of the planning legislation from 1909 up to the present. But we should all be aware that private planning preceded legislative planning by hundreds of years. The schemes created under common law of landlord and tenant and the law relating to restrictive covenants, have produced some of the most beautiful developments in this country—parts of Westminster, Bloomsbury and Bath, for example. Indeed, some of our most beautiful urban development—parts of Oxford, Cambridge, Chelsea and Hampstead, for example—would never have been permitted under our present planning legislation.

There is an essential difference between private and public planning. The private planner has to act under the stimulus of competition. Somebody else might come along and do the job better if he does not do it as quickly and as efficiently as he can. But when we look at the public planner of a new town, we find that he is cocooned from first to last in a suffocating featherbed of statutory protection. It is worth mentioning that a short time ago the present Minister of Housing and Local Government (Mr Greenwood) drew attention in another context to this difference between private and public enterprise. He made the point in connection with Direct Labour organisations (for housing purposes) of local authorities that 'the private builder fails or thrives on the principle of paying for his own mistakes', and urged local authorities to try to reach the standards of efficiency attained by good private enterprise.

Similar examples are not hard to find within the context of planning new towns. When we look at landholdings today, what do we find? The Land Commission, after its first year of operation, has had to confess that it could find almost no privately-owned land available for development being held off the market. Yet this was the *raison d'être* for the creation of the Land Commission. On the other hand, if we look at some of the public landholdings we find a different picture—something like a new mortmain. We find development land under-valued; land held back from development for too long or grossly under-used. I would say that if a lot of this public land were in private ownership it would have been subject to a take-over bid for development long ago.

I should like to enlarge on my remarks about the planner's 'featherbed of protection'. What do the public corporations have that private corporations do not? What is the true economic picture?

First of all, the New Town Development Corporations have compulsory purchase powers. Any private developer would be green with envy at this alone. But the Corporations not only have compulsory purchase powers for the land for their new town; they have these powers for all their ancillary services as well— water, gas, electricity, sewerage, etc. Although in using these compulsory purchase powers a New Town Corporation has now to pay something like the market value (I say 'something like' because we all know that it is a rather hypothetical market value), it must be remembered that all the land for the existing new towns was acquired under a totally different code. For all land put into the acquisition pipeline up to 1959 the compensation paid under that earlier code was derisory compared with the market value which a private developer would have had to pay. This is one example of the hidden subsidies which bolster new town development.

Then there is a startling list of exemptions from the ordinary statutory controls. Exemption from the Rent Acts is perhaps one of the most important. What private developer would not like to have such exemption? But there are others: exemption from advance payments under the Private Streets Work Codes; exemption from Betterment Levy under the Land Commission Act; special protection in relation to enfranchisement under the Leasehold Reform Act; power to extinguish highways, private easements and so on over land they acquire. This is the climate in which new towns are operating, and it is for this reason that I maintain that they are not on an economic basis. I do not say we should not have them; but we should know how much we are paying for them.

In addition to these particular exemptions there are other benefits enjoyed by new towns. They can borrow money at favourable rates of interest. They get direct ministerial grants and indirect grants (for the purpose of providing housing) transferred from the local authority. Working within this framework of statutory protection it is not surprising to hear the claim made that the new towns have paid for themselves. Of course they have! But suppose that a private developer had been able to work within that climate. It is difficult to envisage the sort of riches he might have amassed in that time or what sort of services he might have provided. I am not against the planning of new towns by public enterprise, but their true cost ought to be known, and this is not readily apparent while all these hidden as well as overt subsidies exist.

The private developer enjoys none of these advantages. On the contrary, he suffers from a number of handicaps. His schemes have to go through the administrative planning process and it has been estimated that for any major private enterprise development this is likely to take all of three years. It is difficult to guess the full cost of this in terms of time, money, services, etc., but it must be very considerable. Furthermore, the private developer has to find his way through the web of planning restrictions, and here he is in a much worse position than his counterpart in America. Mr Rouse comes from a country where the philosophy of planning is one of expansion. In Britain it is essentially one of restriction, and it is in this climate that the private developer has to work. The Town and Country Planning Acts constitute probably the most complete system of control that has ever existed in this country or anywhere else in the world. But apart from the Planning Acts, there are many other overlapping codes that also affect the private developer—Housing Acts, Public Health Acts, Highways Acts, Licensing Acts and so on. Many planning decisions are over-restrictive, sometimes they are prejudiced, usually they are arbitrary (because planning has to be arbitrary), always they cause delay. Planning officials are not directly and financially accountable for the consequences of their decisions. Moreover, even where compensation is payable under the existing code of planning, it often bears no relation to the loss suffered by reason of a planning refusal or the imposition of onerous conditions. What possible relevance can an 'unexpended balance of established development value' fixed about 20 years ago have today?

The Land Commission has stated recently that there was a

need for some relaxation of planning policies before it could operate on a useful scale. How many private developers would underline that! But the path is not towards a relaxation; it is towards a tightening up. An example of this can be seen in the Town and Country Planning Bill of 1968 with its modification of the four-year enforcement rule. Furthermore, the rule, first enacted in 1947, that a refusal is deemed if no planning decision is given in two months is an indirect incitement to administrative delay.

But, despite all these handicaps, the private developer can still do many things better than the public corporation. The private developer acting under the spur of competition is likely to be motivated by a much greater sense of financial urgency and therefore committee work and other delays are likely to be pruned to a minimum. Also, because he has a lot at stake, he is highly sensitive to the requirements of the market and of the ordinary individual. The public developer tends to impose his own ideals on the people for whom he is planning. The private developer is likely to give the public what they want: the public developer is more likely to try to give the public what he thinks they should have and this inherent 'do good' element inevitably generates unconscious resentment among the people who are going to live in the place. This is a very difficult thing to control. Once wide planning powers are conferred, it is almost impossible for the planner to know where to stop; what might be called a 'mandarin syndrome' seems to develop in whoever is in charge. The private developer, on the other hand, is out of pocket unless he provides something nearer to public demand.

The new Town and Country Planning Bill envisages wider public participation in planning and the Skeffington Committee is looking into this question, but I do not think that genuine public participation is possible. It will probably give wider scope for participation by the 'hard-core' objectors and the organised groups; but these bodies have always been able to have their say. The ordinary member of the public may not be sufficiently articulate or knowledgeable or have the time and resources really to participate in the planning process. The only way in which he can make his wishes felt is by what he buys or patronises or where he goes. The results can be seen in the failure of public development to anticipate the ordinary whims of the individual, particularly in relation to places of entertainment, the coffee bars and clubs, restaurants and pubs, and so on. The private developer is much more likely to anticipate and meet social needs of this kind.

Planning there must be; but statutory planning, legislative planning, compulsory planning, under the Acts, has frustrated enterprise so much that it has tended to destroy the dynamism of the market forces. The removal of a very great part of it would certainly inject a very considerable vitality into our development and our economic life, and we very badly need this. Only then can we possibly see the true cost of the services we want to provide.

IV. Constraints on the Freedom of the Profit Motive

MARIAN BOWLEY

Professor of Political Economy, University College,
University of London

It might be helpful to try to bring together some of the issues that have been discussed. It seems to me that we have, first, the extreme view that private enterprise can and ought to provide new towns anywhere and everywhere. Secondly, we have the view that private enterprise cannot provide new towns of a socially acceptable character anywhere at all. Thirdly, the view that private enterprise really cannot do anything at all in this country because of controls, subsidies to public authorities and so forth and so on.

What I am going to suggest is that we have to live with the world as we know it to some extent and that in talking about the constraints which need to be and should be applied to the profit motive in new town development, we have to take into account the purpose of new towns in this country, the whole conspectus of regional and social planning and the relationship between new towns and the rebuilding of the great conurbations. The complexity of this situation is reflected partly in the ambiguity about the new towns in this country. Nobody knows to whom they belong or to whom they are meant to belong. At the moment the taxpayer is the owner of the equity in most new towns. Any profits that may turn up on the whole proceeding go back to the Treasury. This is one of the issues which I think has to be considered in relation to private development. (By private development I mean private enterprise acting as complete developers of new towns. The problem of fitting in private enterprise under the umbrella of a public plan is a different and I think a much easier one.)

First, let us look at the new towns and profit possibilities. The first point is that they differ. Some new towns have reasonable profit possibilities. Others have, I think, exceedingly doubtful ones. The new towns in the development areas in North East England, South Wales, proposed new towns in Northern Ireland,

and so on, have an economic future which is probably dependent upon the success of regional economic policy. And against this there is still a question mark, so that from the private enterprise point of view, the issue may well be not of any new town but of just a few new towns holding out profit prospects.

Further, this location and housing policy involvement means that many new towns are not built basically where many people want to live. A new town in the middle of an area of outstanding beauty such as West Sussex would probably be an immensely profitable proposition no matter who undertook the development. Another point is that the occupational structures and income distributions of new towns differ and are likely to continue to do so, so that to talk about an overall uniform proportion of houses for sale is, I think, nonsense. The proportion of owner-occupied to rented houses may be much higher in a place like, say, the future Milton Keynes than in Cumbernauld. So again the opportunities for private enterprise are likely to differ.

The interaction between location of industry policy and new towns is likely to affect the detailed prospect of individual new towns very much. The problem of assessing profit prospects can thus be exceedingly complex, the answer depending on a great number of general factors affecting the location and type of new town. While on the whole location of industry policy probably improves the prospects of new towns in the least prosperous areas, it can (as the recent example of Cwmbran shows) have disastrous effects even within a less prosperous area.

Second, an overall constraint on profitability is that, like it or not, a great part of the infra-structure of new towns is provided as a social service and a large proportion of the housing is provided, and is likely to continue to be provided, at uneconomic rents for a variety of reasons, some good, I think, and some bad. A certain proportion of the families in this country are not prepared or are not able to pay consistently an economic rent for the type or standard of housing that the community has selected—and I think this is very important. Most people can pay for a 'butt or a ben' of the old highland type but the type of house, Parker Morris or what-not, that is now the standard for new construction is a very different proposition. A large chunk of housing in new towns is therefore going to have to be on a non-profit basis. This I think has been accepted in discussion by many people, and an impor-

[44]

tant question arises, if private enterprise is to take the full responsibility for developing new towns—that is, undertake the development, get out the plan and control the plan basically. It may well be that the community will wish to charge them a fee or levy, because it is perfectly clear that the community will itself have to pay for a large section of what is included in the plan, including both infra-structure and the subsidies to rented dwellings.

It may also mean that the community is left with the unprofitable new towns and private enterprise has the most profitable new towns.

There is thus another uncertainty as to the relationship between such profits as are available in new towns for development and the extent to which private enterprise should be required to share those profits with the public interest, however defined. Such uncertainty is likely to cast an atmosphere of gloom over the whole procedure although it may not be regarded by all potential developers as an insuperable obstacle.

So much for general profit prospects. I want lastly to touch briefly on the technical points concerning the general reasons which lead to constraints on the private developer's right to maximise his profits. The first and most familiar is that the time-period over which public and private interests are concerned to maximise beneficial profits can be different. The rates of discounting may be different, the community may discount future benefits at a lower rate than the private sector. So there is a possibility, and I think it must be taken into account as normal, that public and private interests can diverge very frequently in matters of planning and land use.

Second, even when these particular reasons for divergence between private and public interest may not exist, experience has shown that development based on profit maximisation may involve economic and social costs which will fall on the community in whole or in part and not on the developer. Unqualified optimism that the criteria of private profitability and public social and economic interest in town development will automatically coincide can only lead, I suggest, to disillusionment, particularly where the developer occupies a position of monopoly power. Frank acceptance of the probability that even 'enlightened' self-interest will differ from the public social and economic interest

[45]

from time to time, together with the introduction of appropriate constraints, is more likely to provide a reasonable basis for the utilisation of the resources and initiative of private enterprise in this sphere. Some prior agreement on areas of constraint and on questions of ultimate ownership of assets would seem to me to be more useful than an attempt to deal with the problem in terms of, say, some limitation of the rate of profit. My suggestion would be to find the conditions under which profit could be allowed to be maximised and then let private enterprise, if it will accept the conditions, go ahead and maximise its profits; but this means a very much more careful analysis of conditions than has yet been made.

It seems apposite to conclude with a quotation from a pamphlet by one Thomas Manley who was concerned with the rebuilding of London after the Great Fire. The pamphlet, 'Usuary at 6% examined', was published in 1669 and in it Thomas Manley was discussing the effect of a rate of interest of 6 per cent on the profits of speculators, or, shall I say, developers. He wrote:

'The present interest of money . . . can be no just scare-crow to the Builders since all Builders I have yet conversed with may have eight, nine or ten per cent and very good Rents for their ground besides. As for those who are to build in the worst, and by-places, they are to build the meanest Houses and so what they fall short in Rent will be saved in Building. . . .'

There is something for everybody there I think. There is something specifically for the builders in the last bit I want to quote, which I think indicates the magnificent optimism which is traditional of the building industry. Manley wrote:

'I will appeal to all the world if the rebuilding of London goes not on much faster than could be reasonably imagined by him that shall consider the very discouragements the Builders have laboured under, as fears of enemies abroad, doubts at home, wars and rumours of wars; fears, jealousies, . . . scarcity of materials, dearness of workmen, peevishness of neighbours; grounds and concerns inter mixing differences between land-lords and tenants and the like; many whereof being overcome by the prudence of his Majesty . . . the work goes so happily on, that by the blessing of the Lord I doubt not to see that City within three or four years the joy of her Friends, the envie of her enemies and the beauty of Christendom.'

[46]

V. Problems of Obtaining Private Capital for New Towns

NATHANIEL LICHFIELD

Professor in the Economics of Town Planning, University College, University of London

Professor Bowley has discussed a theoretical economic framework for the profit motive of private capital in new towns. I am going to elaborate some of the points she was making on the basis of the financial appraisals of cost and return I have made in recent years of several new towns, including the private enterprise new town of Cramlington in County Northumberland. I cannot reveal specific figures but will generalise from them.

It is helpful to think of a new town as a comprehensive package of four constituents: the purchase of the land, and the construction of the infra-structure (main roads and utility services), social overheads (schools, churches, community centres, which do not directly earn money), and finally, of the buildings—commercial, residential, industrial—which do earn direct rents. The building of a new town recognises that a combination of public and private agencies are necessary to provide the four constituents. In our public new towns we have, of course, the Development Corporation, central government, local government and the nationalised boards in the public sector and private enterprise, normally as ground lessees or 'rack renters'; in the private enterprise new town of Cramlington the only real difference is that, instead of a public corporation, you have a private development company. There is still a mix of public and private agency. This leads on to the first simple point: there is really no such thing as a private enterprise new town if by this is meant 100 per cent private investment. This must also be so in the United States—even in Columbia. The private development company is not of itself out of its profits seeking to build, for example, all the main sewers and the main utilities. Thus even an American private enterprise new town is, I guess, a mixture of public and private agencies.

The interesting point for this Conference is thus really the balance of the mixture, and the extent to which this mixture can be increased towards private enterprise. A few figures will help. In a study of some of the London new towns as at 1961, Professor Wendt and I forecast that on completion the element of private enterprise would be of the order of 20 per cent.[1] With some of the more recent new towns, the proportion of private enterprise in a Corporation new town could rise to, say, 30 or 40 per cent, and there is a general target of 50/50, in housing at least. In Cramlington the element of private enterprise is certainly moving beyond that, but it has not reached 100 per cent.

The second point to make is one of principle: from the figures, and ignoring inflation, it is doubtful—more than doubtful—whether if private enterprise were to undertake a 100 per cent investment in the new town it could make any net profit at all. More precisely it is doubtful whether the value of the completed development would be more than the initial cost of the investment. Put another way, it is unlikely that the real rise in land value over initial land acquisition costs would be such as to compensate for the capital investment in bricks and mortar that you put into the town in order to reap the rise in land value. Of course with inflation, which raises money values more than money costs, the situation could be different.

So we get to the third point: in any new town that is a mixture of public and private enterprise, the infra-structure and the social overheads must to a large degree be financed out of rates and taxes, and not out of the rents from the revenue-producing development.

Therefore, if you are going to build a comprehensive new town, some kind of partnership is necessary between the public and the private agencies.

In the specific private enterprise element which, by definition, as Professor Bowley has pointed out, must be profit-earning, the next question is: can the private sector make a profit, a surplus of revenues on sales or rents over costs? The short answer, based on our studies, is 'Yes'. The new towns around London which Professor Wendt and I studied could make rates of return on their revenue-producing investment over and above the cost of capital, depreciation allowance and the outgoings. The rate of return would not be such to excite a property developer, but it would be

[1] Nathaniel Lichfield and Paul F. Wendt, *Six English New Towns: A Financial Appraisal* (to be published).

significant, particularly if he could visualise a rate of return on equity, that is, borrow the bulk of the capital at going rates of interest in the market with the profit calculated on the residue of the private capital put in. Therefore, in simple terms, money can be made out of the private sector element of a new town, given the private and public mix. This will not be a surprise to those who follow the New Town Development Corporation annual accounts but, and it is a very big but, the profits made by the New Town Corporations owe a great deal to inflation.

This evidence was based on a study in 1962 but we have to recognise that the private sector is moving into greater and not lesser difficulties in terms of making money out of their part of the new town. First, the land cost is higher. The original new towns were started at a time when the Corporations could buy at existing use-value. They are buying at market value, including an element of development value, which eats into potential profits. Another innovation is the betterment levy, which takes a proportion of the development value. Interest rates are, of course, very high today compared with a few years ago. When we did our study, the average interest to be paid by the towns, we thought looking forward to completion, was no more than 6 per cent. Anybody starting today would contemplate as a minimum 7-8 per cent over a long period, and must also take account of the share in equity profits expected by lending institutions. Finally there is Corporation Tax, which would directly affect private development companies.

Generally speaking, we are thus moving into a grimmer phase in terms of private sector development, and all development companies know this when they discuss urban renewal and other developments. We also have to think in terms of another factor which is gloomy for the private sector, and which has been touched on by Professor Bowley. The atmosphere in this country is such that we have moved strongly away from the old-fashioned idea that the public sector pays for non-remunerative development out of rates and taxes, and leaves the profits to the private sector. Over recent years this principle has been departed from in urban renewal, and we have the familiar concept of partnership agreements whereby the authority expects that, if there is any money to be made over and above a normal risk rate of return, it will have a share. I myself think this is a wholly defensible and sensible

[49]

point of view. To those in the private sector who might think otherwise, I would argue that they cannot carry out their projects without the powers and planning powers of the authorities, and furthermore that there is no better insurance to a private investment, whether it is in urban renewal or in a new town, than the willingness of the local authority, the local planning authority and the Minister to secure that their project will be developed in accordance with an agreed plan, which implies that the competitive designs and schemes will be controlled by planning machinery. There is also the point that the authorities are contributing infra-structure and social overheads at the cost of rates and taxes without which the town could not be built at all.

Finally, I would like to look to the future to see how we could foster private enterprise participation in new towns; and I ought to make it clear that I would like to see more private sector participation, if only because it does introduce diversity, variety and more brains and talent into the business. What could be done?

First, any land purchase, not only by a public agency but also by a private agency for a new town, must be geared to a level of acquisition cost which excludes the potential development value to be created. Second, it is a great disadvantage to any investing institution, whether in the private or public sector, to have to spend money before it is necessary, because you merely build up interest on the money lying idle: our studies show that this is a very significant factor in eating away potential profits. Private enterprise new towns in America do this. We in this country have a way round the problem. By designation of a new town we are, in effect, saying that when we need to buy the land we are going to buy it at the level of development value ruling at the time of designation — give and take a little. I would like to see this concession made available in a private enterprise new town so that the private developer himself does not have to invest millions before the need arises merely to avoid paying for development value which his activities will create.

Third, there must be an agreement between the private and public sector—the planning and local authorities and the private developer—on the basis of a financial appraisal which forecasts the cost and return to all the agencies. Out of this comes an agreement on what the private sector ought to get for its venture and what the public sector ought to get for its support. This requires an agreement on such matters as the town plan and programme that the public sector will put in the infra-structure as it is wanted, and that the private sector will follow with its commitments. I think this is the essence of the partnership agreement.

Moving on, I would like to think that in an officially approved private enterprise new town there could be a moratorium from the general situation on betterment levy and corporation tax, not for ever but until the end of an agreed programme of work. And, finally, there are miscellaneous arrangements which could be introduced. For example, if the government were able to guarantee the repayment of money lent by the institutions for an officially approved private enterprise new town, the advance of capital would be stimulated because the government would be taking part of the risk. I would like to see the lending institutions allow the bridging finance to accumulate and not have to be paid out of the receipts in the early years which inevitably lag behind the deficits, and the leasehold system used so that it is the initial developers who will get the benefits of the rising ground rents, which are lost in America through sales; even in the leasehold system there are ways in which capital can be raised without selling off land.

In summary, there is no such thing as a complete private or public enterprise new town, but there is a good prospect for increased participation of private capital in the building of new towns. There is the basis for the private and public sectors getting together. Each side knows what it wants, what it must have. With a properly thought out plan, programme, allocation of agency responsibility and financial appraisal and agreement, it is possible to set up a combined partnership arrangement that can build the new towns. That is what I am hoping is going to happen in Cramlington.

IEA Publications

RESEARCH MONOGRAPHS

1. *Restrictive Practices in the Building Industry* FRANK KNOX and JOSSLEYN HENNESSY (7s 6d)
2. *Economic Consequences of the Professions* D. S. LEES (7s 6d)
3. *A Self-financing Road System* G. J. ROTH (10s 6d)
4. *Marketing for Central Heating* CHRISTINA FULOP & RALPH HARRIS (6s)
5. *Private Enterprise and Public Emulation: A study of Italian experience with IRI and lessons for Britain's IRC* MARIO DEAGLIO (6s)
6. *John Stuart Mill's Other Island: A study of the economic development of Hong Kong* HENRY SMITH (5s)
7. *Source-book on Restrictive Practices in Britain.* Introduced by GRAHAM HUTTON, with a Bibliography by JOSSLEYN HENNESSY (15s)
8. *Universal or Selective Social Benefits?* ARTHUR SELDON and HAMISH GRAY (10s 6d)
9. *The Political Economy of Nuclear Energy* DUNCAN BURN (21s)
10. *Copyright and the Creative Artist: The protection of intellectual property with special reference to music* DENIS THOMAS, with a prelude by A. T. PEACOCK (6s)
11. *Planning in Britain: The Experience of the 1960s* GEORGE POLANYI (12s)
12. *Economic Sanctions and Rhodesia* TIMOTHY CURTIN and DAVID MURRAY (7s 6d)
13. *Consumers in the Market* CHRISTINA FULOP (10s 6d)
14. *Taxation and Welfare* ARTHUR SELDON (7s 6d)
15. *Integration in Freight Transport* A. A. WALTERS (12s)
16. *Dependency and the Family* MARJORIE BREMNER (7s 6d)
17. *The Shape of Britain's Tariff* SIDNEY J. WELLS (7s 6d)
18. *The Cost of Council Housing* HAMISH GRAY (7s 6d)

RESEARCH REPORTS

Choice in Welfare 1965: Second Report on Knowledge and Preference in Education, Health Services and Pensions RALPH HARRIS and ARTHUR SELDON. 1965 (5 gns)

A Competitive Cinema TERENCE KELLY with GRAHAM NORTON and GEORGE PERRY. 1966 (30s)

Economics, Town Planning and Traffic D. J. REYNOLDS. 1966 (30s)

Choice in Housing F. G. PENNANCE and HAMISH GRAY. 1968 (3 gns)